# Alex II
## MAGNUM FORCE

# Alex II
## MAGNUM FORCE

PENGUIN BOOKS

PENGUIN BOOKS

Published by the Penguin Group
27 Wrights Lane, London W8 5TZ, England
Viking Penguin Inc., 40 West 23rd Street, New York, New York
10010, USA
Penguin Books Australia Ltd, Ringwood, Victoria, Australia
Penguin Books Canada Ltd, 2801 John Street, Markham, Ontario,
Canada L3R 1B4
Penguin Books (N Z ) Ltd, 182–190 Wairau Road, Auckland 10,
New Zealand

Penguin Books Ltd, Registered Offices: Harmondsworth,
Middlesex, England

These cartoon strips appeared first in the *Independent*
This collection first published in Penguin Books 1989
1 3 5 7 9 10 8 6 4 2

Made and printed in Great Britain by
Hazell Watson & Viney Limited
Member of BPCC plc
Aylesbury, Bucks, England

## FOREWORD

The most precious gift of all is the gift of laughter. As a recently-married merchant banker working in the arduous and uncertain clime of the City of London; still more as a father-to-be about to usher a new life onto this Earth, poisoned and desecrated by its tenant Man, I find increasingly laughter is a very precious gift indeed.

So it is with shoulders wearied from shaking that I lay down the work I have just perused. The idea that you wish me to write the foreword to a paperback book which is to retail at a price so low that (excuse me whilst I dab a tear of mirth from my eye with a British Airways First Class complimentary "Freshen Up" square) one would still receive change even if one was to tender the lowest denomination banknote in circulation, I find truly risible.

Indeed I shall treat myself to one final chuckle before asking my secretary to place your letter in the automatic shredding machine.

Yours sincerely,

ALEX

**Alex**
PEATTIE + TAYLOR

WHEN I FIRST BOUGHT MY HOUSE IN NORFOLK TEN YEARS AGO I THOUGHT I'D MADE A MISTAKE...

THE PLACE WAS A COMPLETE BACKWATER. THE ONLY PUB IN THE VILLAGE WAS FULL OF YOKELS TALKING ABOUT SHEEPDOG TRIALS AND ARTIFICIAL INSEMINATION. I FELT VERY ALIENATED FROM THE LOCALS...

I WAS EVEN THINKING OF SELLING IT, BUT IN THE LAST SIX MONTHS PROPERTY VALUES IN THE AREA HAVE SHOT UP BY 30%.

THAT MUST HAVE BEEN A RELIEF.

...DOUBLED IN VALUE...

I RECKON MY OLD BARN MUST BE WORTH NIGH ON £60,000 NOW...

WELL LET ME TELL YOU... WHEN I SOLD MY TOWN HOUSE IN ISLINGTON...

...OFFERED ME £75,000...

**Alex** — PEATTIE + TAYLOR

TIMMS, I BELIEVE YOU RECEIVED A CALL FROM A HEADHUNTER THIS MORNING.

WHAT MAKES YOU SAY THAT?

DON'T TRY TO PLAY THE INNOCENT. YOU TOOK A CALL AT 10.27 IN WHICH YOU RECEIVED A JOB OFFER FROM A GERMAN BANK INVOLVING PROMOTION, A £20,000 SALARY INCREASE AND AN UPGRADED COMPANY CAR.

YOU REPLIED THAT YOU WERE QUITE HAPPY WHERE YOU WERE AND TERMINATED THE CONVERSATION.

HOW DO YOU KNOW ALL THIS?

BECAUSE IT WAS ME ON THE OTHER END OF THE PHONE. IT'S A LITTLE TEST I OCCASIONALLY DO ON PEOPLE.

OH!

...WHEN I SUSPECT THE EDGE MIGHT BE GOING OFF THEIR AMBITION.

COLLECT YOUR CARDS FROM MY SECRETARY ON YOUR WAY OUT.

---

**Alex** — PEATTIE + TAYLOR

AT THIS DINNER PARTY LAST NIGHT THE CONVERSATION CAME ROUND TO THE TERRIBLE STATE THE NATIONAL HEALTH SERVICE IS IN...

OH DEAR.

AND SUDDENLY I FELT QUITE EMBARRASSED AND UNCOMFORTABLE ABOUT HAVING PRIVATE MEDICAL INSURANCE.

YOU'RE NOT THINKING OF CANCELLING IT, ARE YOU?

NO, BUT I WONDER IF THERE ISN'T SOMETHING I COULD DO ....LIKE BECOMING A REGULAR BLOOD DONOR.

YOU THINK IF YOU DO MORE FOR THE N.H.S. IT MIGHT ALLEVIATE YOUR GUILT?

NO, I THINK IF I HAD LESS BLOOD IT MIGHT ALLEVIATE MY BLUSHING...

Peattie 315

**Alex**
PEATTIE + TAYLOR

I HEAR THE POLICE HAVE LAUNCHED INVESTIGATIONS INTO IRREGULARITIES DURING THE BROMEX TAKEOVER.

YES. ONE OR TWO TOP CHAPS UNDER SUSPICION APPARENTLY.

...IT EVEN LOOKS AS IF OLD BUFFY FROBISHER HAS FOUND HIMSELF IN A SPOT OF BOTHER WITH THE AUTHORITIES.

MY WORD.

YES. FIRST THING HIS WIFE KNEW ABOUT IT WAS WHEN A COUPLE OF P.C.s ARRIVED AT HER FRONT DOOR ONE MORNING...

POLICE CONSTABLES FROM SCOTLAND YARD?

NO. POSTCARDS FROM BOLIVIA.

**Alex**
PEATTIE + TAYLOR

IF IT WASN'T EMBARRASSING ENOUGH HAVING STARTED TO COME TO CHURCH ON SUNDAYS JUST BECAUSE WE'RE GETTING MARRIED HERE..

...I'M SURE THE VICAR CAN'T FAIL TO HAVE NOTICED THE SWELLING AROUND MY MIDDLE...

WELL, YOU'RE THE ONE WHO INSISTS ON BEING SO SECRETIVE, PENNY

I'M PREPARED TO BE QUITE OPEN ABOUT IT. THE CHURCH IS QUITE LIBERAL THESE DAYS. IT ACCEPTS THAT OUR GENERATION HAS DIFFERENT CUSTOMS.

PASS ME THE 'LIFESTYLE' SUPPLEMENT WILL YOU, PENNY.

SHHH. NOT SO LOUD.

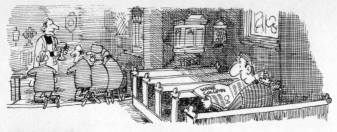

# Alex
### PEATTIE + TAYLOR

IT'S A GOOD THING FOR ALL OF US THAT YOU HAD THAT PORTABLE BREATHALYSER ON YOU, ALEX.

HANDY LITTLE GADGET, EH?

YOU KNOW, IF I HADN'T SEEN THE READING ON IT I'D NEVER HAVE BELIEVED CLIVE WAS IN THAT STATE.

OH, I COULD TELL IMMEDIATELY...

I NOTICED HIS HANDS WERE SHAKING... PLUS, THERE WERE ONE OR TWO OTHER LITTLE TELL-TALE SIGNS...

LIKE THE WAY THE POT PLANT NEXT TO HIS SEAT WAS WILTING.

...AFTER THIS, ANOTHER PENAL PINT DOWN IN ONE FOR TRYING TO AVOID DRINKING ON MY STAG-NIGHT.

**Alex** PEATTIE+TAYLOR

WHEN I SEE SOME OF THESE VILLAINS COMING THROUGH HERE, I HAVE TO QUESTION THE SYSTEM WHICH DEALS WITH THESE PEOPLE, TREVOR...

THAT'S RIGHT, JOHN.

WATCH OUT THERE'S A THIEF ABOUT

THEY GET PUT AWAY IN SOME OVERCROWDED VICTORIAN INSTITUTION, AT MASSIVE EXPENSE AND I REALLY WONDER WHAT IT TEACHES THEM...

...IT SEEMS TO ME THEY MAKE A LOT OF UNDESIRABLE CONTACTS IN THERE AND THEN COME OUT AFTER A FEW YEARS, TOTALLY INSTITUTIONALISED AND WITH EVEN LESS RESPECT FOR THE LAW...

AND THEY GO BACK AGAIN AND AGAIN...

...WELL I DID BUMP INTO BUFFY FROBISHER ON OLD BOYS DAY IN 1986 BUT HE DIDN'T SAY A WORD ABOUT A TAKEOVER...

INTERVIEW ROOM

YES, ONE GETS VERY CHIPPY ABOUT PUBLIC SCHOOLS IN THIS JOB, TREVOR.

**Alex** PEATTIE+TAYLOR

LOOK SUPERINTENDENT, MIGHT I KNOW EXACTLY WHAT I'M BEING CHARGED WITH?

CERTAINLY, SIR...

WE HAVE A RECORDING OF A CALL MADE FROM YOUR CARPHONE TO SIR REGINALD FROBISHER ON MARCH 17th 1987 IN WHICH YOU MENTION THE ROLE OF DIE ERSTE OESTERREICHEN SPURIUS BANK IN THE TAKEOVER...

LOOK, IF I HAD BEEN INVOLVED IN ANYTHING SHADY I WOULD HARDLY HAVE DISCUSSED IT ON THE PHONE. BESIDES, I REMEMBER I STATED CLEARLY THAT I KNEW NOTHING OF IT.

QUITE THE CONTRARY SIR AND THIS FORMS THE BASIS OF OUR FIRST CHARGE...

...DRINK-DRIVING.

...DIE OSHTER... ER...OSHPERRECHSH ...OH YOU KNOW...

AHEM.

**Alex**
PEATTIE + TAYLOR

DON'T OPEN THAT HAMPER, CLIVE – IF YOU'LL TAKE MY ADVICE.

BUT IT'S MY PICNIC, ALEX. I PACKED IT SPECIALLY...

BIP BIP BIP

WELL I'VE JUST RUN MY PORTABLE BOMB DETECTOR OVER IT AND I'M TELLING YOU THERE'S A LIKELIHOOD THAT THIS COULD BLOW UP IN YOUR FACE.

BUT THERE WAS NO BLEEP OR FLASH OR ANYTHING...

EXACTLY.

I HAVE REASON TO BELIEVE YOU MAY BE CARRYING...

... PLASTIC CUTLERY.

BLAST.

**Alex** — PEATTIE + TAYLOR

**Panel 1:** WELL, PENNY, MY BROTHER GREGORY IS COMING TO STAY FOR A FEW DAYS.

I THOUGHT YOU HATED YOUR BROTHER.

**Panel 2:** I DO, PENNY. I DESPISE HIM.

OH COME ON, ALEX. I SAW THAT SMILE OF PURE JOY LIGHT UP YOUR FACE WHEN YOU PICKED UP THE PHONE...

**Panel 3:** A PURELY REFLEX REACTION, PENNY: A MOMENTARY THRILL OF EXCITEMENT AS I HEARD THAT FAMILIAR NONCHALANT DRAWL...

GREG'S?

**Panel 4:** NO, MY OWN, WHEN I HEARD MYSELF TELLING THE OPERATOR I WOULD ACCEPT A REVERSE-CHARGE CALL FROM AFGHANISTAN.

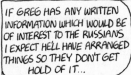

**Alex** — PEATTIE + TAYLOR

**Panel 5:** DO YOU THINK GREG WILL HAVE ANY PROBLEMS GETTING WHAT HE'S WRITTEN OUT OF AFGHANISTAN?

NOT REALLY...

**Panel 6:** IF GREG HAS ANY WRITTEN INFORMATION WHICH WOULD BE OF INTEREST TO THE RUSSIANS I EXPECT HE'LL HAVE ARRANGED THINGS SO THEY DON'T GET HOLD OF IT...

WHERE WOULD IT BE HIDDEN?

**Panel 7:** IN LENGTHY DESCRIPTIONS OF THE AZURE SKIES OVER KABUL... IN TEDIOUS LIGHT-RELIEF PASSAGES ABOUT THE PROBLEMS OF A FOREIGN CORRESPONDENT FINDING A FAX MACHINE IN ISLAMABAD...

**Panel 8:** GO ON... YOU'RE JUST GETTING TO A GOOD BIT...

ER IT'S OKAY, COMRADE. MUSTN'T LET YOU MISS YOUR FLIGHT, EH?

When a woman you've never met before...

**Alex** PEATTIE + TAYLOR

FEELING BAD THIS MORNING, CLIVE?

DREADFUL. THAT REALLY IS THE LAST TIME I GO OUT DRINKING WITH YOU AND THE BOYS FROM METROBANK.

YOU WERE TAMPERING WITH MY DRINKS WEREN'T YOU? I SHOULD HAVE GUESSED WHEN YOU KEPT BUYING ALL THE ROUNDS...

GOD KNOWS WHAT THAT STUFF I WAS DRINKING WAS...

ALCOHOL-FREE LAGER, I SUPPOSE.

PRECISELY.

WE DECIDED WE WERE BORED WITH THE WAY YOU ALWAYS PASS OUT AFTER THREE PINTS AND THEN HAVE TO MISS THE AFTER CLOSING-TIME CURRY SESSION.

THAT LAMB KORMA WAS A SCORCHER.

**Alex** PEATTIE + TAYLOR

PENNY, I BELIEVE SEX WILL ALWAYS BE A PROBLEM FOR YOU IF YOU CAN'T LEARN TO LET GO A LITTLE...

YOU'RE FAR TOO UPTIGHT. THERE SHOULDN'T BE ANY GUILT OR WORRY.

YOU'RE PUTTING UP BARRIERS AROUND YOUR BEHAVIOUR... IF YOU ARE EVER GOING TO FEEL FULFILLED SEXUALLY YOU MUST FIND WAYS TO LET YOURSELF EXPRESS YOUR NATURAL INCLINATIONS...

I WASN'T REALLY IN THE MOOD TONIGHT, ALEX.

HMMM?

**Alex** PEATTIE + TAYLOR

THIS ISN'T A REAL CITY CRIME, ALEX. IT'S JUST AN OLD-FASHIONED BUSINESSMAN RUNNING A SHADY INVESTMENT OPERATION.

THE REAL INJUSTICE IS HOW HIS SORT ALMOST ALWAYS GET AWAY WITH IT...

HOW'S THAT?

BY TAKING ADVANTAGE OF ELDERLY PEOPLE WHO HAVE A BIT OF MONEY BUT VERY LITTLE KNOWLEDGE OF THE MODERN FINANCIAL WORLD, WHO CAN EASILY BE CONFUSED WITH SPURIOUS TECHNICAL JARGON...

...AND WHAT EXACTLY IS A "PERSONAL ORGANISER"?

**Alex**
PEATTIE + TAYLOR

OH, WHEN YOU GO TO THE LOO, CLIVE, YOU'LL NOTICE WE'VE CHANGED OUR USUAL BRAND OF TOILET TISSUE FOR SOMETHING MORE ECOLOGICALLY SOUND..

OH? THE RECYCLED STUFF?

YES.

WELL, WHEN ONE THINKS HOW THOSE LATIN-AMERICAN COUNTRIES, ALREADY BESET BY CRIPPLING INFLATION AND FOREIGN DEBTS, ARE CUTTING DOWN THEIR PRECIOUS RAINFORESTS JUST TO SATISFY THE WESTERN DEMAND FOR LOO PAPER...

IT SEEMS AN APPALLING WASTE, AND IT'S UP TO THE PRIVATE CITIZEN TO TAKE ACCOUNT OF THIS.

URUGUAYAN PESO BANKNOTES?

YES, AND I HAD THESE LEFT OVER FROM A TRIP TO BRAZIL...

**Alex**
PEATTIE + TAYLOR

OH I ALWAYS CARRY SOME OF THEM IN MY HANDBAG. YOU'VE GOT TO BE SO CAREFUL THESE DAYS...

IT'S ALL PART OF THE NEW MORALITY AND RETURN TO OLD VALUES. ONE HAS TO TAKE A RESPONSIBLE ATTITUDE TOWARDS CASUAL PARTNERS..

YES. YOU JUST CAN'T BE SURE ABOUT THEIR PASTS.

MOST MEN AREN'T OFFENDED, BUT IT'S STILL EMBARRASSING AT THAT CRITICAL MOMENT WHEN YOU'VE JUST STARTED GOING OUT WITH SOMEONE AND YOU HAVE TO SAY "ER, DO YOU MIND WEARING ONE OF THESE..?

RESTAURANT

ER...DO YOU YOU MIND WEARING ONE OF THESE?

A TIE? ON MY DAY OFF? BLIMEY, PIPPA, BUT IT WILL REDUCE MY PLEASURE.

**Alex**
PEATTIE + TAYLOR

SURELY YOU'RE NOT GOING BACK TO ALEX, PENNY?

HE NEEDS ME, CHLOE. HE PHONED EARLIER. HE SOUNDED VERY DOWN.

IT HADN'T OCCURRED TO ME THAT MY LEAVING HIM WOULD CAUSE HIM ANY DISTRESS BUT HE TOLD ME HE'D HAD TO TAKE A LOT OF TIME OFF WORK RECENTLY... HE'S REALLY VERY UPSET.

IT SEEMED RIDICULOUS: HIM SITTING THERE AT HOME; ME MOOCHING ABOUT AIMLESSLY HERE. BOTH OF US MISERABLE. SO I'M GOING BACK.

WELL IF YOU'RE SURE YOU'RE DOING THE RIGHT THING...

PENNY! THANK GOD YOU'RE BACK! RIGHT: THE NEW FUTON IS BEING DELIVERED AT ABOUT 11 O'CLOCK... THEN AT 3 I WANT YOU TO LET IN THE MAN TO FIX THE DISHWASHER...

OKAY. SEE YOU LATER, ALEX.

**Alex** — PEATTIE + TAYLOR

IN THIS INSTANCE IT SEEMS ROUTINE PHONE MONITORING BY THE BANK REVEALED THAT A CORPORATE FINANCE JUNIOR HAS PASSED PRICE-SENSITIVE INFORMATION TO A FUND MANAGER...

NOW OBVIOUSLY WE ALL KNOW THE POWER OF THE LAW TO DEAL WITH INSIDER TRADING, BUT FRANKLY THE CITY COULD DO WITHOUT THE ADVERSE PUBLICITY THIS GENERATES...

PROPER SELF-REGULATION WOULD AVOID ANY REPETITION OF THIS EMBARRASSING SCANDAL ...IT IS ESSENTIAL TO LAY DOWN INTERNAL GUIDELINES AS TO HOW TO DEAL WITH PEOPLE LIKE THIS...

LIKE, FROM A PHONE BOX FOR A START..

...AND PREFERABLY EMPLOYING SOME SORT OF CODE NAME...

**Alex** — PEATTIE + TAYLOR

ALEX, DID YOU KNOW THAT IN SOME PLACES IN THE BRITISH ISLES THEY PUMP UP TO 40 MILLION GALLONS OF UNTREATED HUMAN SEWAGE INTO THE SEA EVERY DAY?

ASTOUNDING, ISN'T IT?

FACTS LIKE THAT SHOULD BE BETTER PUBLICISED..

...IF WE WANT OUR CHILDREN TO GROW UP HEALTHY AND NORMAL.

...WHEN I THINK HOW RACKED WITH GUILT I WAS FOR YEARS BECAUSE I ONCE SECRETLY WEE'D IN THE SEA AT MARGATE...

A DROP IN THE OCEAN, CLIVE.

# Alex
### PEATTIE + TAYLOR

I CAN'T BELIEVE HOW YOU'RE TAKING THIS, ALEX... PENNY'S 20 MINUTES LATE AND YOU'RE JUST CALMLY SITTING THERE PUTTING THE FINISHING TOUCHES TO YOUR SPEECH...

ACTUALLY I NEED THIS EXTRA TIME TO POLISH IT UP, CLIVE...

THERE'S REALLY NOTHING TO WORRY ABOUT YET... IT'S TRADITIONAL FOR THE BRIDE TO BE LATE FOR HER OWN WEDDING...

BESIDES, I'VE STATIONED CAROLINE OUTSIDE THE CHURCH AND SHE'LL LET ME KNOW IF THERE'S ANYTHING AMISS.

RING RING

THEY'RE GETTING A BIT IMPATIENT, ALEX...

I'M ALMOST FINISHED, CAROLINE. SEND THEM THROUGH IN ABOUT FIVE MINUTES...

TAP TAP

SPEECH

**Alex**
PEATTIE + TAYLOR

Memo: From Alex to Clive.
Re: Meal with Japanese clients.
Japanese hospitality is very formal and may sometimes be overwhelming...

At all times remember Japanese hosts go to a great deal of trouble to provide for the comfort and pleasure of an "honoured guest"...

and it is considered impolite for a guest not to show his appreciation of these efforts...

Hint:- As you enter the room you should notice the traditional Japanese flower arrangements and miniature ornamental trees that are set about the room for your sake.

...FOR MY SAKE.? I'D BETTER REMEMBER THAT.

MORE SAKE, CLIVE?

OH. LOVELY. YES PLEASE!

# Alex
PEATTIE + TAYLOR

WHERE DID CLIVE RUSH OFF TO, BRIDGET?

BACK HOME TO CHECK OUR NEW ANTI-BURGLAR SYSTEM...

IT TURNS THE LIGHTS IN THE HOUSE ON AND OFF AT RANDOM TO GIVE THE IMPRESSION THERE'S SOMEONE AT HOME BUT CLIVE COULDN'T REMEMBER IF HE'D SWITCHED IT ON OR NOT

AH... HE'S BACK...

BAD NEWS, BRIDGET. I FOUND A WINDOW BROKEN...

YOU IDIOT... SO YOU HAD SWITCHED IT ON...

ER YES... SORRY, BRIDGET.

HOW MANY TIMES DID I REMIND YOU IT'S "TRICK OR TREAT" NIGHT?..

... AND THEY'D SPRAYED "MEANIE LIVES HERE" ON THE FRONT DOOR...

EXCUSE ME... HAVE YOU SEEN MY GLASSES?

OVERTAKER!

UNDERTAKER.

# Alex
PEATTIE + TAYLOR

I ALWAYS FIND ATTENDING THESE CHARITY FUND-RAISING BALLS A VERY EDUCATING EXPERIENCE...

IN OUR DAY-TO-DAY LIVES I THINK IT SOMETIMES ESCAPES OUR ATTENTION THAT NOT EVERYONE IS FORTUNATE ENOUGH TO ENJOY ALL THE ADVANTAGES OF OUR AFFLUENT LIFESTYLE..

AND AN EVENT LIKE THIS MAKES ONE AWARE OF THE EXISTENCE OF PEOPLE LESS PRIVILEGED THAN ONESELF.

LIKE JARVIS... DID YOU NOTICE HIM BIDDING IN THE AUCTION FOR THE PORTABLE TELEPHONE?

I CERTAINLY DID. DO YOU THINK THAT MEANS HE HASN'T GOT ONE?

**Alex** PEATTIE + TAYLOR

IT'S ALMOST MIXED. PASS ME THE COCKTAIL GLASS.

OH ALEX. I DON'T KNOW IF I WANT ONE OR NOT NOW.

SHAKE SHAKE SHAKE

YOU'RE ALWAYS SO RUDE ABOUT ANYONE YOU SEE WITH ONE IN THE PUB... MAYBE YOU'RE RIGHT ABOUT THEM BEING NASTY VULGAR STICKY THINGS...

THEY GIVE ME A BIT OF A HEADACHE THAT'S ALL.

LOOK AT THAT LOVELY PINK COLOUR.

WELL, ARE YOU GOING TO HAVE ONE OR NOT?

ER... LET'S SEE...

PINK...YES I AM... I'M GOING TO HAVE A BABY.

GOOD. NOW I CAN THROW OUT THIS GHASTLY COCKTAIL SET YOUR AUNT SOPHIE GAVE US...

INSTRUCTION LEAFLET

INSTANT PREGNANCY TEST.

**Alex** PEATTIE + TAYLOR

WELL PENNY, THIS HAS ALL COME AS RATHER A SHOCK.

THERE WE WERE- WE'D JUST DONE ALL THE CHARTS AND PLANNED TO START TRYING FOR A BABY NEXT MONTH...AND NOW IT TURNS OUT YOU'RE ALREADY PREGNANT.

AREN'T YOU PLEASED?

OF COURSE I AM, OVERJOYED... IN FACT I'LL PHONE EVERYONE STRAIGHT AWAY AND TELL THEM THE GOOD NEWS...

PLICK PLICK

JUSTIN? ALEX HERE. GUESS WHAT?... I WILL BE ABLE TO TAKE THOSE CLIENTS TO THE OPERA ON THE FOURTH OF NEXT MONTH AFTER ALL...

**Alex** PEATTIE + TAYLOR

I CIRCULATED A MEMO TO THE FLOATING RATE NOTE TEAM SUGGESTING THAT THOSE WHO WANTED TO DO WELL IN THE CITY MIGHT BENEFIT FROM AN 'OUTWARD BOUND' COURSE.

YOU KNOW, WHEN YOU GET DROPPED IN EXMOOR WITH JUST A TIN OF SPAM AND A BOX OF MATCHES TO SURVIVE FOR A WEEKEND.

YES.

I THOUGHT IT WOULD BE A GOOD TEST OF THEIR INITIATIVE AND DECISION-TAKING... SORT OUT THE LEADERS FROM THE WIMPS.

FIVE OF THEM WENT ON IT.

I HEAR ONLY HODGES SHOWED HE WAS MADE OUT OF THE RIGHT STUFF.

THAT'S RIGHT. HE JUST LAUGHED AND THREW THE MEMO IN THE BIN.

**Alex** PEATTIE + TAYLOR

NOW PENNY, ARE YOU SURE YOU SHOULD BE DRINKING THAT?

ALEX! ONE LITTLE LAGER SHANDY CAN'T HURT.

IT'S NOT YOU I'M THINKING OF, PENNY. IT'S THE BABY... THESE EARLY WEEKS ARE AN IMPORTANT STAGE FOR THE GROWING FOETUS...

AND I CONSIDER IT VITAL THAT ALL THE EMBRYONIC FACULTIES OF OUR CHILD SHOULD BE AFFORDED THE BEST CHANCE OF FULL DEVELOPMENT...

... INCLUDING A DISCERNING PALATE. HERE... HAVE SOME OF THIS 12 YEAR OLD MALT.

**Alex**
PEATTIE + TAYLOR

WHAT'S THIS, CLIVE?

A BLOCKBUSTING DOCUMENTATION OF A MAN'S RAMPANT SEXUAL APPETITE.

THIS AMERICAN AUTHOR HAS WRITTEN ABOUT HIS EXPERIENCE OF HUNDREDS OF ONE-NIGHT-STANDS AND HOW IT MADE HIM REALISE THE FUTILITY OF BEING A COMPULSIVE WOMANISER.

IT'S A BEST SELLER IN FOURTEEN COUNTRIES AND HE'S ALREADY WORKING ON ANOTHER... I'D LOVE TO KNOW WHAT SOMEONE LIKE THAT MAKES IN THE WAY OF ADVANCES.

"HELLO BABY, WANNA BE IN MY BOOK"?

OVERGROUND

WAY OUT →

GOLF CLUB BAR

♪ RAIN DROPS KEEP FALLING ON MY HEAD... ♪

**Alex** PEATTIE + TAYLOR

YOU'RE A BIT LATE THIS MORNING, ALEX.

YES. THE TUBE I WAS ON WENT OUT OF SERVICE AT WEST BROMPTON.

THIRD TIME IT'S HAPPENED THIS MONTH. THIS TIME THE PASSENGERS WERE SO EXASPERATED THAT THEY DIDN'T JUST GET OFF MEEKLY WHEN THE GUARD TOLD THEM TO. THEY ARGUED WITH HIM AND REFUSED TO MOVE.

IT WAS A WONDERFUL SIGHT. ALL THOSE NORMALLY RESERVED COMMUTERS SITTING STUBBORNLY IN THEIR PLACES AND REFUSING TO BUDGE. THEY SHOULD ALWAYS ADOPT THAT DEFIANT APPROACH.

WHY? DID THEY GET THE TRAIN MOVING?

I SHOULDN'T THINK SO, BUT I WAS ABLE TO GET A TAXI WITHOUT THE USUAL SCRUM.

**Alex** PEATTIE + TAYLOR

IT'S VERY DEPRESSING, CLIVE. I'VE SPENT A FORTUNE OVER THE YEARS KEEPING APACE WITH THE LATEST DEVELOPMENTS IN HI-FI SOUND QUALITY...

FIRST ONE HAD TO HAVE A PLANER-3 RECORD DECK, THEN A COMPACT DISC PLAYER, AND NOW I'LL HAVE TO SHELL OUT OVER £4,000 FOR A DIGITAL AUDIO TAPE PLAYER. THIS REALLY IS THE LIMIT.

25" T.V.

NEW FROM JAPAN D.A.T.

BUT ALEX, REMEMBER D.A.T. IS A TOTALLY NEW SYSTEM THAT PRODUCES PERFECT SOUND REPRODUCTION QUALITY.

PRECISELY.

D.A.T.

SO PRESUMABLY THERE'S NEVER GOING TO BE ANYTHING MORE EXPENSIVE.

GOSH... YOU'RE RIGHT.

**Alex**
PEATTIE + TAYLOR

...IF YOU'RE STILL APPREHENSIVE, SIR, I WILL PERSONALLY CHECK OVER ALL THE RELEVANT AREAS OF THE AIRCRAFT.

THANK YOU STEWARDESS.

YOU'VE A RIGHT TO BE CONCERNED, ALEX.

EVEN THE MOST CAREFUL MONITORING MAY HAVE FAILED TO DETECT ACTIONS PERPETRATED BY SOMEONE IMPERSONATING ONE OF THE AUXILIARY STAFF, CLIVE...

I MEAN, ONE HAS READ STORIES OF JOURNALISTS WHO'VE MANAGED TO SMUGGLE DUMMY BOMBS INTO AIRCRAFT BAGGAGE HOLDS BY MASQUERADING AS TOILET CLEANERS...

I'VE THOROUGHLY CHECKED THE FIRST CLASS LOOS, SIR, AND YOU CAN REST ASSURED THEY'RE SPOTLESS AND FULLY EQUIPPED WITH THE COMPLETE RANGE OF EAUX DE TOILETTE AND AFTERSHAVES.

THAT'S A WEIGHT OFF MY MIND.

**Alex**
PEATTIE + TAYLOR

GOOD EVENING...THIS IS YOUR CAPTAIN SPEAKING...WE HAVE ONE PASSENGER WHO HAS NOT SHOWN UP FOR THE FLIGHT AND, AS HE HAS CHECKED IN LUGGAGE, I'M AFRAID WE SHALL HAVE TO FOLLOW EMERGENCY PROCEDURE.

WHAT?!

ALL THE BAGGAGE IS BEING UNLOADED ONTO THE TARMAC. PASSENGERS ARE REQUESTED TO DISEMBARK AND POINT OUT THOSE ITEMS THAT BELONG TO THEM...

I DON'T BELIEVE IT. HOW INFURIATING.

BUT ALEX...WE'RE ONLY GOING OVER TO PARIS. WE DON'T HAVE ANY BAGGAGE.

EXACTLY...AND I'VE JUST BOUGHT A BRAND-NEW SET OF LOUIS VUITTON MATCHING SUITCASES.

# Alex
PEATTIE + TAYLOR

IT MAY BE A CLICHÉ TO SAY IT, CLIVE, BUT THEY REALLY ARE THE BEST DAYS OF YOUR LIFE – THE TIME ONE SPENDS UP AT OXFORD...

OH, I AGREE..

CRITICS WILL SAY IT'S TIME SHAMELESSLY DEVOTED TO HEDONISM AND SELF-INDULGENCE... AND THERE'S A MEASURE OF TRUTH IN THAT.

YES.

BUT WHERE'S THE HARM? AFTER ALL IT'S ONLY A RELATIVELY SMALL FRACTION OF ONE'S LIFE THAT ONE SPENDS IN THIS IDYLL.

PRECISELY.

GRADUATE RECRUITMENT WEEK ONCE A YEAR... A COUPLE OF DAYS DURING THE SUMMER... IT'S NOT EXCESSIVE...

YES. AND HOW MANY OTHER BASTIONS OF PRIVILEGE ARE THERE WITH SO MANY PEOPLE ON PALTRY 4-FIGURE INCOMES WHO'VE NEVER SEEN A PORTABLE TELEPHONE?

---

# Alex
PEATTIE + TAYLOR

WHAT OUR BANK WILL BE LOOKING FOR IN GRADUATE RECRUITMENT WEEK IS HARD EVIDENCE OF YOUR ACHIEVEMENT, AMBITION AND GENERAL SUITABILITY TO A CAREER IN THE CITY...

THIS APPLIES FROM THE FIRST INFORMAL INTERVIEW WHEN WE LOOK OVER A CANDIDATE'S CURRICULUM VITAE, TO THE FINAL IN-DEPTH EXAMINATION ON THE BASIS OF WHICH A JOB OFFER MAY BE MADE.

BUT AT THIS INITIAL STAGE WE ARE NOT OVERLY DEMANDING. WHEN STUDENTS CAME UP FOR INTERVIEW LAST YEAR I BELIEVE ONLY 2 CVS WERE REJECTED OUT OF HAND...

...THOUGH IT'S UNLIKELY THAT ANYONE WHO HAD ARRIVED IN A SKODA OR A LADA WOULD HAVE GOT MUCH PAST THE DOOR EITHER.

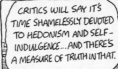

**Alex**
PEATTIE + TAYLOR

I'M SORRY, ALEX BUT THIS CANNOT BE ALLOWED TO CONTINUE.

PARDON?

YOU'VE BEEN RUDE, AGGRESSIVE AND SARCASTIC TO THE LAST SIX CANDIDATES WE'VE INTERVIEWED. I'M OBLIGED TO SAY I THINK IT'S MOST UNFAIR.

CLIVE, THIS IS RIDICULOUS.

JUST BECAUSE YOU CONSIDER YOURSELF AT AN ADVANTAGE THAT'S NO REASON FOR YOU TO ALWAYS BEHAVE IN AN INTIMIDATING AND DOMINEERING FASHION DURING INTERVIEWS. IT'S TIME YOU TRIED SHOWING SOME CONSIDERATION AND RESTRAINT.

YOU'VE PUT THAT VERY FAIRLY, CLIVE.

...WHICH SHOWS YOU'RE ABSOLUTELY PERFECT AS MISTER NICE.

ALEX, I ABSOLUTELY INSIST THAT I BE ALLOWED TO BE MISTER NASTY THIS TIME.

THUMP THUMP

NEXT!

WHY CAN'T I TAKE A TURN PUNTING?

**Panel 1:** WELL, WHAT AN UNPLEASANT YOUNG MAN.

YES...

**Panel 2:** I SUPPOSE HE THOUGHT HE WAS CLEVER, RUBBISHING ALL THE OTHER CANDIDATES LIKE THAT, BUT I WASN'T IMPRESSED.

NO.

**Panel 3:** I FOUND HIM SNEAKY AND DEVIOUS. I WOULDN'T WANT SOMEONE LIKE THAT WORKING FOR ME.

CERTAINLY NOT..

**Panel 4:** IN THE HIGHLY COMPETITIVE BACKSTABBING WORLD OF MERCHANT BANKING ONE NEEDS PEOPLE WHOSE LOYALTY ONE CAN RELY ON.

TEAM SPIRIT. EXACTLY.

**Panel 5:** LET'S RECOMMEND HIM FOR A JOB IN PATTERSON'S DEPARTMENT.

BRILLIANT.

**Panel 1:** WHEN I SIT HERE IN MY OLD COLLEGE WATCHING THE WAY UNDERGRADUATES ARE WAITED ON HAND AND FOOT BY LACKEYS...

**Panel 2:** ...I CAN'T HELP THINKING WHAT A MOLLY-CODDLED ARTIFICIAL WORLD IT IS FOR THEM.

PROVERBIAL IVORY TOWER, ALEX.

**Panel 3:** I WONDER HOW MANY OF THEM HAVE ANY IDEA OF THE PRESSURES OF REAL LIFE OUTSIDE THE UNIVERSITY.

THEY OBVIOUSLY PREFER NOT TO THINK ABOUT IT.

**Panel 4:** I MEAN, THEY'D BE SACKED ON THE SPOT FOR MAKING SUCH A PIG'S EAR OUT OF SILVER SERVICE WAITING IN ANY NORMAL CATERING INSTITUTION.

WHOOPS. SORRY, SIR.

NOT TO WORRY.

IT'S TRUE IT'S TRUE.

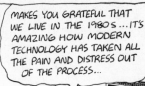

**Alex**
PEATTIE + TAYLOR

I FINALLY WORKED OUT HOW TO GET ALL MY LUGGAGE IN THE CAR.

GOSH! HOW DID YOU DO IT?

WELL, I PUT MY "DYNASTAR" SKIS AND "ROSSIGNOL" MONOSKI ON THE ROOF RACK ALONG WITH MY HAND-CRAFTED LUGE THAT I BOUGHT IN SWITZERLAND LAST YEAR...

RIGHT.

AND I STACKED SOME OF MY LOUIS VUITTON SUITCASES ON THE BACK SEAT AND THEN MANAGED TO SQUEEZE MY "OLYMPUS" SPORTS BAG, WALKIE-TALKIES, SKI BOOTS AND "LOOK" BINDINGS ON THE BACK WINDOW SHELF.

SO I SEE.

AND WHAT HAVE YOU GOT IN THE BOOT?

MY SPONGE BAG.

HOLLOW BONG

**Alex** PEATTIE + TAYLOR

THIS IS A GOOD OPPORTUNITY TO GIVE YOU A REVISION TEST ON YOUR HIGHWAY CODE, PENNY.

OH GOOD.

RIGHT... WHAT DOES THE SOUNDING OF THE HORN INDICATE?

ER... LET'S SEE... THE HORN MUST NEVER BE USED AS A REBUKE...

...BUT ONLY TO INDICATE "I AM HERE" TO OTHER ROAD USERS...

YES... AND WHAT ELSE?

ER... THERE ISN'T ANYTHING ELSE...

TUT TUT, PENNY...

PAARP

IT ALSO INDICATES: "I HAVE FORGOTTEN MY PERSONAL CODE NUMBER WHICH I HAVE TO KEY IN WITHIN 17 SECONDS TO STOP MY CAR ALARM ACTIVATING"

PAAAARP!

DAMN... ER 4361... NO... THAT'S MY CASHPOINT NUMBER.

ANK GOLF DAY

**Alex** PEATTIE + TAYLOR

GOODNESS, CLIVE... WHAT A TEE SHOT.

THWACK

PING

I HOPE YOU HAVEN'T FORGOTTEN THAT IT'S RUPERT YOU'RE PLAYING NEXT WEEK... AND WHEN ONE PLAYS THE BOSS A CERTAIN – SHALL WE SAY – DECORUM MUST BE OBSERVED.

PING

PLAYING LIKE THAT YOU'RE LIABLE TO CAUSE AN UPSET.

YOU MEAN YOU THINK I MIGHT BEAT HIM?

NO, I MEAN YOUR INCOMPETENCE IS SO UNBELIEVABLE, HE'S BOUND TO THINK YOU'RE DELIBERATELY LETTING HIM WIN.

PLOP